I LIKE BROWNIES BETTER
THAN WHITEFISH

Happy Munching!

Roberta

I LIKE BROWNIES BETTER
THAN WHITEFISH

ROBERTA WEISNER

Rutledge Books, Inc.   Danbury, CT

Rutledge Books, Inc.
107 Mill Plain Road, Danbury, CT 06811
1-800-278-8533
www.rutledgebooks.com

Manufactured in the United States of America

Cataloging in Publication Data
Weisner, Roberta

I Like Brownies Better Than Whitefish

ISBN: 1-58244-174-X

1. Non Fiction. 2. Short Stories.

Library of Congress Control Number: 2001097529

Dedicated to my best friend,

whom you'll read more about later,

and to my family circle of love

Contents

THE AFFAIR 1

PRE-SHAPE UP 3

50 — IMPOSSIBLE! 7

EXCUSE ME, SIR 10

DON'T GET IT 12

KIDS — EASY; HOUSE — IMPOSSIBLE .14

I'M OLD ENOUGH TO WEAR WHAT I'M
      COMFORTABLE IN OR AN ODE TO A SWEATSUIT 16

THE MANTRA 19

A FRIEND REMARKED TO ME TODAY .21

THE TRICKS 24

I'LL TELL YOU A LITTLE SECRET 26

I'LL START MONDAY 29

TOO HUMID 31

TICKTOCK 33

BEST FRIEND 35

7-11 37

59+. 39

A SUMMER AFTERNOON 41

THE SHOPPING LIST 43

THE HAT 46

NEVER 48

SOMETIMES 50

MAN OVERBOARD 52

MY GRANDMOTHER 55

THE CUSTODIAN 58

MUMBLE-JUMBLE 60

WEAR GLASSES 62

MOVIE SET 64

GEOMETRY 65

A PLEASURE 68

IT'S RIDICULOUS 70

LOOK, LOOK! 72

U.P.S 74

ANGEL DUST 76

THE CIRCLE 78

GROW BABY GROW 80

MILLIONS 81

MONDAY MORNING 84

WHERE, OH WHERE? 85

COUNTING SHEEP 87

THE ULTIMATE HOUSE GIFT 89

HIS WORST NIGHTMARE 91

I'LL TEACH YOU A NEW WORD 93

SALUTE 95

OUT OF THE MOUTHS OF BABES AND OTHER
        RANDOM THOUGHTS 97

DID I HEAR RIGHT? 101

THE BROKEN-DOWN TRUCK 103

THE SEARCH 105

200 DEGREES 107

BUSTED 109

HALT 111

HELP! 112

HIGHER EDUCATION 114

I CAN'T STAND IT 115

NOT THAT BAD 117

OH NO 118

PASSÉ 120

SHUT UP 122

STRAIGHT OUT OF PARIS. 124

THE INTRODUCTION 126

THE LATEST 127

WHO SAID WHAT 129

YOU CAN TELL 130

ROMANTIC INTERLUDE. 132

"THE BELLS ARE RINGING FOR ME AND MY GAL" 135

P IS FOR 137

CALIFORNIA HERE I COME 140

The Affair

We had been married twenty-six years and I still only had eyes for my husband. But one day:

I was in a crowded room and saw him.
My pulse raced and my heart beat faster.
At the same moment I was laughing at my self for my reaction.
I felt like a magnet was drawing me to him. All I wanted to do was to be alone with him and put my arms around him.
How was that possible?
I didn't know him.
I had just seen him for the first time minutes ago.

Finally, we were alone in the room.
I crossed the space quickly and embraced him.
Feelings of love—that's all I knew.

The Affair

I counted the days until I could see him again.
It's been six years now.
When I'm not with him, I think about him.
We never part without making plans to meet again.

If I'm on the phone and he calls, I hang up.
I can't wait to hear his voice.
When he kisses me and tells me how he loves me, I melt.
Oh! The joy of a first grandchild!

PRE-SHAPE UP

I recently came back from one of the well-known beauty and fitness spas in the country. It is also known for its wonderful hikes.

Little did I know I was in for emotional and physical anguish.

Mealtime was a joke. My mantra of the week was not, "peace", "calm", "sea", or "blue". My mantra was, "Are you going to finish that? If not, pass it down." I would eagerly await the next course only to be told, "That's it. You just had the whole meal."

The topic of conversation wasn't any better. Everyone lamenting how they couldn't zip up their size 4s and had to (they couldn't bear to say the number) buy size 6. I was also a 4, when I was four, and a 6, when I was six.

"Oh well," I thought, "tomorrow will be the equalizer. I've been walking four miles several times a week for years. I'll leave these out-of-shape weaklings in my wake."

The hike leader went to the front of the dining room and proceeded to recite the following day's hikes:
1) Advanced hike—6:00 A.M.—straight vertical—15 miles
2) Intermediate—6:15 A.M.—semi-vertical—12 miles
3) Beginner—6:30 A.M.—slight vertical and straight—10 miles

I burst out laughing at the joke and immediately realized I was the only one laughing. The joke was on me.

I think quickly, though, in moments of stress and I started to limp as I got up from the dining room table. "What's wrong?" I was asked. "Oh," I said, "I was jumping rope for two hours and I guess I overdid it!"
I fretted all night. How was I going to keep up? I shouldn't have lost sleep over it. There was no one to keep up with! I was the only one in the beginner group.

I slowly walked two miles and then told the leader I shouldn't push myself any further on a twisted ankle. I then tried to look teary as I said, "I was so looking forward to the fifteen-mile vertical hike. Perhaps next season."

The mortification of my life was the last afternoon. I walked into the dining room thinking perhaps there were some crumbs on the floor I could lick up. I really wanted to go through the trash cans, but I thought it might be a tad tacky.

I had to rub my eyes—thinking it was a mirage—but there was

actually a plate of cookies in front of me. "How lovely," I thought, "They're making plates of cookies for each table."
No salt, no sugar, no fat. Egg whites and air. About ten calories each. "OK," I thought, "I couldn't eat that disgusting weed salad for lunch (about 200 calories) so if I eat all twenty cookies, it's the same thing." Well, isn't it?

That night the twenty of us sat down to our 1/4-inch piece of whitefish, but visions of last night's dessert was filling us all with glee.

Then the chef appeared. "Ladies," he said, "I made you a delicious, delectable delight for your last night here. A dish of one hundred-calorie treats, loaded with salt, sugar, and fat. Unfortunately, they are missing."

The gasps of horror were louder than their anger; they had lost their most precious jewels.

Everyone looked at everyone else. I stood up and said, "I stole the cookies from the cookie jar." It wasn't enough that I was humiliated; I also consumed two thousand calories.

If they had trophies for the slowest, most tired, exhausted, hungriest and thighs that you could pinch an inch, I would have walked away with all the prizes. As it was, I left feeling depressed, dejected and out of shape.

I'm looking for investors to open a pre-spa. A place where women are gradually eased off thousands of calories a day, and serves desserts that you can identify.

Pre-Shape up

The walks start at nine and will be slow enough to smell the flowers.

Anyone under size 10 will be barred at the door.

Wanna come?

50 – Impossible!

I'm turning 50—it can't possibly be.
Maybe all my friends, but certainly not me.
But then again, I needed my glasses to write this
because I can't see.

I would love to jog five miles instead of my fast walk.
But I can't—because my knees make me balk.
The young guys all pass me by.
It's to my daughters they want to say "Hi."

In high school my friends and I discussed what we each
were going to wear on Saturday night.
Now our conversation is we want to get our cholesterol
down with all our might.

Four-inch spike heels were always for me.
But now I wear a low flat—how can that be?
I used to be able to sleep around the clock.
Now my eyes open every few hours in the dark.

Wasn't it just yesterday that my three daughters learned to
reach their hands out to me?
I'm turning fifty—how can that be?

Camp—sweet sixteen—senior prom—college
Were all just a few years ago to me.
I'm turning 50—how can that be?

My doctor, my lawyer, my dentist, and my beautician are all
younger than me.
I'm turning 50—how can that be?

The president and congressmen have always been decades
older than me.
But Clinton wasn't—how can that be?

I used to go to bed at night anticipating all my sweet dreams.
But now I must remember to put on my night cream.
I just saw dental floss and a gum massager on my makeup table.
It must be for my grandmother—certainly not for me.

I was startled the first time I was called ma'am.
But now I don't give a damn.

Everyone says I look like 40.

I have the energy of 30.

But inside I know I'm really 10.

Because at the beach, I love to play.

Kicking my feet in the sand and water all day.

On the dance floor, I can outlast any kid.

I still glide through the water like a fish.

I walk along the lake each morning.

I hit a tennis ball with spin.

In two minutes I can pen a pretty good line.

So all in all, I'm doing pretty fine.

My daughters all love to talk and confide in me.

And they agree, "Mom—50! You can't be!"

My husband looks at me and says it's a twenty year old

he still sees.

So 50—I can't possibly be.

When my grandson sees me he says not "Grandma", but

"Mom-Mom."

So 50—I can't possibly be.

I'm richer than any Arab princess or Ivana Trump could be.

Because of my beautiful family that surrounds me.

But wait—I just came back from my walk and a good-looking

Yuppie tried to flirt with me, or as this generation says,

"hit on me."

So maybe 50 is not so bad to be!

EXCUSE ME SIR

Many years ago, when I was a youngster, I lived in a building where I was the only child. After further exploring, it turned out that I was the only little girl on the entire block.

One day, I was playing with my tea set when my mother noticed I had set my play table for three guests. "Honey," she said, "do you want Daddy and me to have tea and cookies with you?"

"Oh no!" I replied. "I'm going to drink tea with Higo and Ditz."

"Higo and Ditz!" she exclaimed, "Who in the world are they?"

"Can't you see them?" I answered. "They are my two best friends!"

She quickly realized that I had created two imaginary best friends to fill that void in my life. I would walk down the street with my palms out, like I was holding their hands.

One day my mom and I got on the bus. We were sitting on the long bench in front. On the next stop a man got on and started to sit next to me. I immediately said, "Excuse me, sir, but you cannot sit on Ditz."

My mother winked at him and whispered in his ear. He smiled at me and moved down the aisle.

Last week we were on an airport shuttle bus. No air and 110 degrees! A 300-pound man got on with a tank top and proceeded to sit next to me, taking up 3/4 of the seat.

I wanted so badly to say, "Excuse me, sir, but you are sitting on Ditz!"

Don't get it

I belong to a large, beautiful health club in Chicago, which shall remain nameless.

To join you have to be young, waspy, tall, anorexic, with silicone boobs and blonde hair. However, they don't want a discrimination suit, so they had to take one person who was Jewish, middle-aged, short, zaftig, and brunette with natural boobs. Yours truly.

These goddesses exercise while I'm sleeping in the morning and they are still exercising when I go to bed at night. Actually, I don't even have to get on a machine. I get exhausted just watching them!

The thong unitards—my God, my diaper covered more of my tush than that!

I don't know why they bother printing a menu. They all order a petite, fat-free, sugar-free yogurt and then moan and groan about how full they are.

What I don't get, and never will, is the scene in the locker room. Naked—as in stark naked. Now, I don't shower with clothes on, but when I walk out of the shower, I wrap a towel around myself— even in the privacy of my home.

Not these babes! They strut around the locker room like they are dressed to the nines!

The mind-boggling part is when they sit down to blow dry their hair for 30 minutes, legs spread. Get the picture?

I figured out how to fit in to the public areas of the club. I put water on my face, leotard, and hair, and a wet towel around my neck. Then I walk around muttering, "Exhausted. Exhausted. A spoonful of yogurt, please."

But I'll never fit into the locker room scene.

I just don't get it.

KIDS – EASY; HOUSE – IMPOSSIBLE

I recently spent a week watching our grandchildren. Easy as pie—well mannered, did their homework and their carpools were taken care of.

The house was a different story. I didn't need a nanny or cleaning lady. I needed a Ph. D. from Illinois Institute of Technology to assist me.

First of all, I had to learn the code to open the garage. Then another code to open the door. Keys, what are they? I wanted to watch the news—forget it! Each TV required two remote controls and numerous assorted buttons to program.

It was much too cold in the house, but once again it was a computer system, so I settled for a sweatshirt and jacket.

Their microwave (mine is heat, defrost, enter)—beyond me.
I ate the food frozen.

Music-oh, sure—try their CD system! I wouldn't even attempt it; I
hummed to myself.

The video and VCR—I shuddered when I saw the instructions,
so I read a book instead.

It got dark early and I wanted to turn on the outside lights; but
once again it was a computer system. The lights inside were
another complicated program with arrows, buttons, and screens.
Thank God for flashlights.

The phones, oh my! This button for paging your friend in Timbuktu,
that button for call waiting, call forwarding,
conference call, fax, etc. I think I'll send a letter.

I told my grandson to tell his brother dinner was ready. I saw him
walking to the telephone to push various buttons to call him on
the intercom. I accomplished it easier; I yelled, "Eric, dinner!"

By this time my brain was exhausted and I wanted to go to bed.
However, I had to spend the next twenty minutes trying to set the
alarm system. Couldn't do it—slept with my eyes open.

Report card: Kids—Easy
            House—Impossible

I'M OLD ENOUGH TO WEAR WHAT I'M COMFORTABLE IN OR AN ODE TO A SWEATSUIT

The sun wasn't shining
any moment it was going to rain
I wanted to wear a sweatsuit,
but my friend said, "It takes no brains."

"Women don't know what to wear",she said,
"It really drives them insane,
so they throw on a sweatsuit;
it shows they have no brains."

She's right; jeans, slacks, sweater, tights,
vest, blouse, blazer—what a pain!
I long to wear a sweatsuit,
even though it shows I have no brains.

My makeup was on. My hair looked pretty.
I didn't feel at all plain.
I so want to wear that sweatsuit,
but I keep hearing her say,
"It takes no brains."

I have such a long car ride tomorrow
there is not an available train.
I would be so comfy in a sweatsuit,
but does it mean I have no brains?

I feel so good in my sweatsuit,
and I certainly don't look as if I operate machinery or run a
crane.
But alas, I can't possibly wear one
because my friend said, "It takes no brains."

All over the country, from Rodeo Drive to Michigan Avenue,
Fifth Avenue to small-town Maine,
Women the world over wear them,
Do we all have no brains?

Sweatsuits are not flattering—when we wear them it looks like
there has been a definite gain.
Who wants to look fat—maybe she's right
Maybe we have no brains.

When you buy Armani, Urgaro, or Valentino,
your money goes down the drain.

I'm old enough to wear what I'm comfortable in or An ode to a sweatsuit

However, because of all of the above,

I shall run only in Ralph Lauren.

Because I can't ever wear a sweatsuit again

You see, I'm much too vain

and I want to be known as the gal with a brain.

THE MANTRA

A "fat-free" diet is the mantra on the nation's lips
Carry your water and sip, sip, sip.

In boardrooms, shops, and construction sites across the land
From ski slopes to planes, to lying on the sand.

Fat free, fat free, fat free is all we hear
So I said to my husband, "This is for me, my dear."

I have such a yearning for salty, fatty lox
But instead, I ate my fat-free nuts (the whole box).

Apple pie and chocolate cake were on my mind
But the six fat-free brownies taste good, I find.

The mantra

Visions of Fannie Mae candy danced in my head
And the pound of fat-free candy tasted like lead.

A chocolate sundae is what I really wanted to lick
But the quart of fat-free yogurt would make me sick.

Pretzels don't even have one gram of fat
So I finished the bag in no time flat.

Mrs. Field's cookies—I've thought about all day and night
But instead, I ate the fat-free cookies—now there's not one left
in sight.

Hot, buttered popcorn is all I wanted to munch
Instead, I ate three fat-free health bars for lunch.

The cream cheese is fat-free, so on my bagel I put more than
a pinch
Fat-free, fat-free, this diet is an absolute cinch.

A week later I eagerly stepped on the scale
And immediately turned quite pale.

I can't understand why the fat-free diet isn't working for me
I never ate a gram of fat, as you can plainly see!

A FRIEND REMARKED TO ME TODAY

"You used to be my most sophisticated friend and now you're with your grandchildren all day."

I just nodded, but I really wanted to say:

I've loved watching George Solti conduct, but I must admit that I get a bigger kick watching my grandson bang the drums in time to a beat.

I laughed all through the latest Broadway comedy, but I must admit when my grandson imitated a duck's walk, I laughed longer and harder than any line in the play.

I used to marvel at Michael Jordan's prowess on the court, but I must admit when my grandson sinks the ball in his backyard game, I clap longer and harder.

A friend remarked to me today

There is satisfaction and a great deal of self-esteem when I see my words in print. But I must admit teaching my grandson to write his name was the greatest satisfaction of all.

The ballet always has me sitting on the edge of my seat, but I must admit that during my granddaughter's ballet recital I was so sorry that Martha Graham wasn't alive to see my three-year-old protege.

The museums and art galleries have brought me many happy hours, but I must admit that I have never stared at a Miro as I do at the scribble drawing taped to my refrigerator.

Educational TV has given me many informed hours, but I must admit I enjoy watching "Sesame Street" with the grandchildren.

A night at the opera is a marvelous treat, but I must admit singing "It's A Small World" with my granddaughter is so much fun.

Movie reviews, book clubs, I've done them all, but I must admit I far prefer reading Dr. Seuss to the children.

When an article I wrote was well done I felt satisfaction, but I must admit it falls short of the gratification I feel when my grandchildren use new vocabulary words I taught them.

I love a good strong game of tennis, but I must admit when my grandson hits the ball over the net to me, I'm happier than if it was Agassi.

Europe, the Orient, we've done it all, but I must admit I get a thrill showing the children the sights of Chicago.

I have been an avid reader all my life—Shakespeare to Danielle Steele to David Mamet. The words I heard yesterday over the phone, long distance: "Grandma, I sent the rain to Florida so you'll come home; I miss you so much," touched my heart like no writer or poet ever will.

Does this mean I'm not sophisticated anymore?

The tricks

It is imperative, if you love brownies, to know "the tricks".

There can be a dozen brownies on a plate. When my husband falls asleep, I eat twelve. There still will be a dozen when he gets up. He was bright enough to count them, but not smart enough to measure them. I cut each one in half!

If the cookie jar is filled before you go to bed, it's very simple. Eat all the cookies you want, fill the jar with paper towels, and put one layer of cookies on top.

Yesterday, I really had to be creative. There was a huge single chocolate turtle that I resisted for three days. My husband wouldn't touch it because he was testing my willpower. At 3:00 A.M., I caved in. I ate it in one gulp, took a rose from a vase, and replaced it on the plate with a note.

"Honey, I didn't want to eat the turtle, so I wished it would turn into a rose and it did!"

I'LL TELL YOU A LITTLE SECRET

I'll tell you a little secret, but don't ever tell anyone. I have three daughters and my firstborn is my favorite.

The first is always the most special.
The first feel of sunshine after a harsh winter.
The first shower on a hot, muggy day.
The first taste of a freshly baked cookie.
Our first kiss, our first date.
The first time we swam across a pool.

My first daughter is like Mother Theresa—she is sweetness and goodness all rolled together. I can have thirty lipsticks and if I admire her one, she offers it to me. She exudes love and warmth. She kisses her baby hundreds of times a day. She never thinks of herself first, second or third. She does not have strong material desires. When you're with her she always acquiesces to the other person's wishes. She never, ever holds a grudge. She is sensitive and caring. She does not have a selfish bone in her body. She never wants to take time for herself. Every waking hour since her baby was born—two years ago—she has spent with him. She thanks you many times for any little thing. She makes me feel very loved and always wants to be with me.

She's a joy to be with.
Don't tell—she's my favorite.

I'll tell you a little secret, but don't ever tell anyone.
My middle daughter is my favorite.

No stress of raising your first infant.
No stress of the first earache, first chicken pox, and first fall. You're more relaxed and take the time to enjoy the moment, because you know how quickly they grow up.

My middle piddle is Perfection. From her makeup and dress to the way her kids look, to her home to her business. Her way with words is brilliant. Everything she touches is done with class and dignity. From her competitive athletic drive, to her devotion to her family, it is done with the utmost thought, feelings, and loving care.
She always makes the effort to go the extra step. She dotes on her three men and tries in every way—every day—to make them happy.

I'll tell you a little secret

She has the morals and virtues of the highest nature. She makes
me feel very loved and special and always wants to be with me.
She lives each day, but has thoughts and concerns for tomorrow.

She's a joy to be with.

Don't tell—she's my favorite.

You always savor the last.
The last minute of sun on a summer day.
The last vacation day.
The last taste of dessert.
Your last baby.

My youngest is Sunshine.

She radiates laughter and enthusiasm.
She is an optimist.
She has a marvelous sense of humor.
She always sees the glass half-full and never half-empty. She skips
through life and doesn't make a big deal out of things.
She doesn't sweat the small stuff. She doesn't impose rules
and regulations on you. She's a free spirit that soars. People
instantly gravitate to her. The ease with which she walks through
life makes her very easy to be with. She has always
been "Eloise at the Plaza". She lives for today and doesn't fret
about tomorrow. She makes me feel very loved.

She's a joy to be with.
Don't tell—she's my favorite.

I'LL START MONDAY

Every female over five knows what that expression means. It does not refer to learning a new foreign language or training for the marathon.

It's that vulgar four letter word, DIET. You notice the first three letters are DIE. Yesterday being Sunday, I had to stuff myself into oblivion so that I would feel bloated for at least the first few hours of D.D. (Deprivation Day).

I was innocently walking by Dunkin' Donuts and heard my name being called, "Roberta! Roberta!" So what do you do when you're called? You go! Of course upon entering the store, no one was there except the counter girl.

I had a little—OK, medium—OK, large—fix, with skim milk, of course, and started to leave the store. I didn't see the "WET

FLOOR" sign and went sliding across the tile and landed on my wrist.

"Don't worry, Miss," the counter girl said, "we'll call your husband to pick you up."

"Right on!" I said, "Just tell him I'm on the floor of Dunkin' Donuts!!! No thank you, I'll crawl out of here first!"

Today at the health club there were several other women wearing ace bandages and of course they asked each other "What happened to you?"

1st lady: "I fell down the Black Diamond at Snowmass."
2nd lady: "I was rear-ended on the highway."
3rd lady: "Four sets of tennis, every day, for a week."

Now they all looked at me. "So what happened to you?"

I'll be damned, if I was going to say I fell on the floor of Dunkin' Donuts!

"Well, I was delivering Meals on Wheels to the infirm, and I carried too many trays at one time."

Too Humid

My sister and I will be out shopping and she will suggest stopping at Walmart, or Sam's Club, or Target.

Suddenly my body temperature plunges or rises. I beg off going saying, "I'm freezing and it's going to drop even colder." Or in the summer, "I'm dying. I can't breathe. I need a shower." Or if the climate is perfect—I get an instant headache.

Now a friend can suggest going shopping at Neiman Marcus. I can have a 103° fever and suddenly the health fairy waves her wand and I'm fine. There might be a blizzard on Michigan Avenue and I'll ski down the street to get there.

I can't help it. The saleswomen are prettier, Chanel smells better than tacos, and cashmere is softer than polyester.

Too humid

In all due respect to Sam Walton, when I drive by, I hear a lone voice saying, "Go home. Go home." And when I walk by Neiman Marcus, I hear a chorus of glorious voices singing, "Come in! Come in!"

TICKTOCK

The first time I became aware of pushing the clock was during final exam week at college. I remember looking at the clock and wishing it were three hours later.

The next recollection I have of wanting to turn the hands of the clock is when I became engaged. I couldn't wait to be married and spend the rest of my life with the love of my life.

Then pushing, pushing the nine months away (three times in fact) until my pregnancy was over and I could hold the baby.

Pushing, pushing the time. "I can't wait until they sleep through the night—are off the bottle—out of the crib—toilet trained, etc."

Pushing—pushing. "I can't wait until they can walk and talk. I can't wait until the girls are in school all day."

And the reverse.

Pushing—pushing the clock to see them again. "I can't wait until they are home from camp. I wish the kids were home for college break."

Pushing, pushing. "I can't wait for my daughters' weddings."

Pushing, pushing. "I'm going to be a grandmother." Pushing the nine months away.

I woke up this morning. I still feel energetic and healthy and so does my husband.

My three daughters vie to be with me, and my grandchildren still have the desire and time to be with us.

I'm on a mission—a quest—I'm going to buy up all the cement glue in the world so I can stop all the clocks in the universe from ticking.

BEST FRIEND

I've heard the expression "best friend" used so many times
this week.
My daughter telling me that she is planning a vacation with her
best friend.
A neighbor introducing me to her best friend.
A Bears player saying he was happy his best friend was hired
to play for the Bears team.
A columnist writing on the importance of having a best friend.
A friend saying to me, "I'll tell you this secret because you are my
best friend."

My grandson telling me his best friend was coming over to play.
I also go shopping, have lunch, and plan vacations with my
best friend.
I also play with my best friend, tell him my secrets, and my best
friend is always on my team.

Best freind

The best part, though, is that I never have to invite my best
friend over.
I'm married to him.

7 – 11

7-11 is a very successful convenience store chain.

So I decided to open a franchise.

My 7-11, though, is not on your busy neighborhood corner.

Like all stores, mine also opens at 7.

Instead of a storefront, my convenience store is a telephone. One of my three daughters will always call at 7 and one of the three will end the day with a call at 11.

Instead of selling milk, juice and newspapers, I sell advice on children, spouses, friends, business, school, camp, furniture, clothes, diets, trips, etc.

I'm doing a booming business and sometimes I have to stop helping one customer (daughter) because another customer (daughter call-waiting) needs me more.

7 – 11

Last Christmas, during the holiday season, "my store" was busier than ever.

One night the phone rang at 11:45 P.M. and my husband blew his top.

"Calm down," I said, "It's the holiday season and I extended my hours!"

59+

I drive a car 60 miles an hour.

60 people fit on a subway car.

There are 60 Oreos in two bags of cookies.

60 degrees is a perfect temperature.

I could practice tennis my serve 60 times and it would still be terrible.

Sell 60 valuable Beanie Babies and you'll make a lot of money.

Swim 60 laps and you'll be a Class A swimmer.

60 people fit on a train car.

There are 60 minutes in one hour.

Twelve basketball teams have 60 men.

Someone who runs 60 miles can qualify for a double marathon.

60 glasses of water fill a bathtub.

A large box of crayons holds 60 colors.

60 strands of spaghetti would never be enough for me.

I couldn't jog for 60 minutes, but I can walk for 60 minutes.

There are 60 students in two classrooms.

60 people would not fit on an elevator.

There are 60 seconds in a minute.

60 bees would ruin a picnic.

Somehow, some way, 60 gray hairs sprouted on my scalp.

I can't sleep more than 60 minutes without waking up.

Climbing 60 stairs is not as easy as it used to be.

Thirty dimples (sounds better than cellulite!) on each thigh equals 60.

But I just spent 60 exciting minutes watching our grandsons in a soccer match and I smiled a 60-watt smile as the other players' parents told me how well my "sons" played.

I spent 60 exhausting minutes playing tennis with my grandsons and this 60 year old almost beat them. Next time I will!

A SUMMER AFTERNOON

We held hands as we entered the pool.
My left hand had a firm grip on my father.
My right hand lightly held my granddaughter.

My father, a recovering stroke victim, tentatively took his first step
into the water.
My granddaughter, just learning to walk, gingerly took her first
steps into the water.

I helped my dad change out of his bathing suit.
I helped my granddaughter change out of hers.

I put a bib on my dad and cut his meat.
I put a bib on my granddaughter and cut her meat.

I read a foreign affairs article to my dad.
I read Barney to my granddaughter.

I watched the news with my dad.
I watched Sesame Street with my granddaughter.

I put away my father's tennis racquet he will no longer use.
I put away the infant toys my toddler granddaughter will
no longer use.

I put my father to sleep.
I put my granddaughter to sleep.
I cried myself to sleep.

THE SHOPPING LIST

You're going to be a grandmother again.
Words I waited all year to hear.
Just hearing them to my eye brought a tear.

I was so elated I could hardly wait!
I began a countdown for the important date.

I was so thrilled I didn't know what to buy first.
I was so excited I thought I would burst!

It didn't matter girl or boy.
I bought the latest toy.

Cribs, buggies, playpens, and a high chair.
Bottles, diapers, and a comb and brush for his hair.

The shopping list

There wasn't a single item I didn't buy.
My shopping list was a mile high.

As the time drew near I began to pray.
And finally came the blessed day.

The world's most beautiful boy came into my sight.
I'll never forget that thrilling night.

I raised three girls so I'm an expert you see.
Any question I told my daughter, Jami, "Just ask me!"

Pick the baby up—it's time for him to eat.
Get the blanket—cover his tiny feet.
Don't feed him again—he's had too much!
It's almost time for his lunch.

Pick him up—you can't let him cry.
You'll figure out what's wrong-if you just try.

Change him now, of course he's wet.
You want to make a bet!

Can't you tell he needs a nap, my dear?
You can't let him out of your sight, I fear.

He needs to burp—that's easy to see.
I'll do it—just give him to me.

He's still getting up all through the night.
I can tell—you look a sight!

If you hold him every moment he will never want to be
put down.
Put him in the playpen—I say with a scowl and a frown.

Put a sweater on him—he's going to sneeze.
Can't you tell he's starting to freeze?

You're going to breast-feed for a least a year, you say?
When will you have time for a Jami day?

A supplementary bottle would really be neat.
Do you think you can accomplish that feat?

I had my grandchild, I was so glad!
But my daughter began to look sad.

Then one day I realized that the daughter I love so much
I had to let go and release from my clutch.

When I did my shopping there was one item I forgot to buy.
So to all grandmothers—get this and your daughter and daugh-
ter-in-law won't cry.

When my fifteen-month-old grandson is at my daughter's
breast every few hours for a sip
I can't utter a single word—there's adhesive tape on my lip.

THE HAT

I heard the hat calling to me as I entered Neiman Marcus. A large broad-brimmed chapeau covered in black mink. Gorgeous! I hesitated, but my hand immediately whipped out my credit card.

"No box," I said, "I'll wear it out." I put it on and immediately, as I walked through the store, the compliments poured on me and my beautiful chapeau. "Wonderful hat!" "The prettiest I've ever seen!" etc, etc.

I was on my way to a birthday luncheon with a group of friends and I couldn't wait to show off my new acquisition.

I got into a cab and the first words from the driver were, "Lady, great hat youse got on!"

I arrived at the party and the doorman said, "Miss, I wish my wife wore hats like that!"

I stepped into the elevator and the elevator operator said, "Ma'am, that is one fine lookin' hat!"

I sat down to lunch and the waiter said, "A pleasure to wait on a woman dressed like you!"

We spent a lovely two hours discussing politics, travel, family, friends, and gossip. However, it was like the "Emperor's New Clothes"—there wasn't anything on my head but hair. The hat was never mentioned. I found it fascinating that all my "friends" on the street paid me a compliment, but the "strangers" at the birthday lunch never said BOO.

NEVER

"I will NEVER get mad at my child,"
Says the mother with her day-old baby.

"I will NEVER give my child a time out,"
Says the mother with a six month old.

"I will NEVER say no to my daughter; she can have as many
ear pierces as she wants,"
Says the seven year old.

"I will NEVER tell my son to turn down the stereo or clean
his room,"
Says the ten year old.

"I will NEVER tell my kids not to monopolize the phone,"
Says the fifteen year old.

"I will NEVER tell my son he can't have the car or has a curfew,"
Says the sixteen year old.

"I will NEVER tell my kids they have to go to a certain college,"
Says the seventeen year old.

"I will NEVER tell my daughter she can't spend a year traveling
through Europe,"
Says the eighteen year old.

"I will NEVER tell my daughter certain guys aren't right for her,"
Says the twenty year old.

"I will NEVER tell my son he can't skydive,"
Says the twenty one-year old.

"I will NEVER just have two kids,"
Says the unmarried twenty two-year old.

"I will NEVER interfere in my married children's lives,"
Says the forty five-year-old future mother-in-law.

"I will NEVER butt in with the raising of my grandchildren,"
Says the future forty eight-year-old grandmother to be.

I will NEVER be a burden to my children.
I'm sixty.

SOMETIMES

Sometimes my three daughters drive me crazy.

At sometime or another one or two or three of them are on a
diet. I hear the daily reports of how much they've gained or lost
and how frustrated they are.

Sometimes #1 is arguing with #2 or #1 with #3 or #2 with #1 or #2
with #3 or #3 with #2 or #3 with #1. I'm told of every discussion
and why each one is right.

Sometimes they think I'm telling them what to do and they don't
like it.

Sometimes they think I'm interfering with something they say to
their children.

Sometimes they get annoyed with my worrisome nature.

Sometimes they just don't realize that every word that pops out of my mouth can't be the word they want to hear.

But for the few sometimes, I am deluged with thousands of all the times.
All the time—every day—in every way I thank God for my three beauties.

All the time I wake thinking about them and go to sleep thinking about them. Shouldn't be, but their happiness or unhappiness affects my mood for the entire day.

They're my Nobel Prize and my Olympic gold medal.

All the time we love each other with all our hearts.

All the time I know I am blessed to have such wonderful daughters.

MAN OVERBOARD

We went on a cruise recently in South America. It was summer there and the weather was extremely hot and humid. There was no way I could sit all day in the scorching sun, so my husband searched the deck for a spot of shade.

The only shade was where the ice cream bar was so the ice cream wouldn't melt. Is it my fault that my husband put my chaise lounge right next to it?

We decided before we booked the cruise that huge breakfasts and the lavish lunch buffets were not going to be for us. A light breakfast, exercise, skip lunch, and then dinner. All went according to plan until day four and by then I was ravenous.

After all, I had eaten like a monk for four days. I was certainly entitled to a rocky road ice cream with a sugar cone. Don't you agree?

11:00 A.M.—My husband was across the pool, basking in the sun, eyes closed. "Make your move NOW!" I thought. Looking backward over my shoulder to see if he was sitting up, I quickly ordered a rocky road.

1:00 P.M.—Everyone leaves deck for gargantuan Mexican spread. Not us.

1:15 P.M.—Husband is reading paper; his back is to me.

1:16 P.M.—"I'll have another rocky road on a sugar cone, please."

3:00 P.M.—Afternoon tea and cookies. Not us.

3:01 P.M.—Husband goes to the bathroom.

3:03 P.M.—"I'll have another rocky road on a sugar cone, please. Not a double, sir. I'm dieting."

5:00 P.M.—Happy hour. Not us.

5:05 P.M.—Husband goes in the pool.

5:07 P.M.—"I'll have another rocky road on a sugar cone, please."

Man overboard

5:30 P.M.—My husband saunters over and says, "Honey, I have never met anyone with such discipline. You walked three miles this morning, you've swum for an hour this afternoon, and you have not had a morsel to eat. You must be famished! We won't be eating until eight. Come on, I'll get you a rocky road."

"Oh no," I said. "I don't want anything."

"Honey," he said. "You'll faint going from eight this morning until eight tonight!"

We walked over to my favorite haunt and my husband said, "Give this young woman a rocky road."

The waiter said, "Jesus, man, she's had four already!"

My husband started to gasp and turn white, but I couldn't be bothered with him. I was too busy throwing the waiter overboard.

My Grandmother

We live in a mobile society.

Unfortunately, many children just get to see their out-of-town grandparents on holidays.

Even living in the same city, everyone is so busy it can be difficult to make time for your grandparents.

My sister and I were blessed that we grew up living in the same house as my grandmother. We all lived together until we got married.

My sister and I never received a present from my grandmother. It wasn't her style to go to a store and buy a gift. But we received hundreds of more valuable presents all during the year.

I'm embarrassed to recall how many times I didn't make my bed or hang up my clothes. I would come home from school and my room would be spotless.

I never went to a dressmaker until I was married. Every loose button, every torn seam was immediately fixed by my grandmother.

My mouth waters when I think of her frickla. We were out to dinner and the waitress mentioned a wonderful, brand new dessert on the menu. I tasted it and yelled, "It's my grandmother's frickla!" So I guess she was way ahead of her time.

My grandmother never walked through the door of a Michigan Avenue store. She never opened a copy of Vogue. But she was very aware of fashion. She always wanted to know where I bought an outfit and how much it cost. She would then comment on it and it wasn't always a compliment.

She never walked into a health club and certainly didn't know what the expression "working out" meant. However, she was always very proud of being slim and never failed to mention her weight to me.

For most of her life she crocheted slippers. I would buy a dozen at a time from her for $2.00 a piece. She loved having money she earned and as quickly as I gave it to her, she would give it to the nurses at the nursing home.

I told her that a store on Michigan Avenue was selling the slippers. She would always ask me how business was and was very indignant when I didn't buy enough from her.

Many times I would entertain her with stories of my daughters' dates. She would say, "Tell them to wear perfume and skirts. Men don't like pants!"

My grandmother never had a formal education. She taught herself to read and write. Yet her will, her sense of humor, and her ability to weave a story surpassed the most learned of men.

She loved hearing how she "saved my life". I was seriously dating someone—we'll call him Joe. My grandmother saw many traits in Joe she did not like. She would always say, "Joe is not for my granddaughter."

My grandmother lived on the first floor and we lived on the second. One evening I waited hours for Joe and he never showed up. Later that night, I told my parents how shocked I was that he didn't show or call. My grandmother said, "He was downstairs hours ago." I told him, 'Get away, you bum, you are not good enough for my granddaughter!' " Well, that was the end of Joe and soon after, I met my husband.

People have told me that I am a devoted grandmother. I don't take credit for this. It is the only way I know. It is what I have seen my whole life. It is the kind of grandmother I was blessed to have and the kind of grandmother my mother was to our three daughters.

A grandmother who is always there for you is a beautiful legacy to pass from one generation to another.

THE CUSTODIAN

There's a magnificent old maple tree in our yard. Its overflowing branches totally shade our pool. Forty-five summers, since I was a small child, I've begged my father to cut it down.

"Please, Dad, the pool is totally in the shade. I can't get a tan. I'm cold. It's got to be cut down."

Every summer was the same argument and he would always reply, "Not as long as I'm here. That tree is magnificent—it stays."

One day when he went into the city, I called a tree trimmer and had the tree scalped. It looked like a skinned ostrich. When he came home in the evening and saw the tree, he turned white. He barely spoke to me all week.

My dad died a few months ago and my husband was walking around the property with a gardener.

As he approached the tree, I started to heave with racking sobs. "What's wrong?" my husband asked. "The pool is in the shade. The kids want us to cut down the tree."

"Not as long as I'm here!" I cried. "The tree is magnificent. It stays."

Mumble – Jumble

Oh, for the olden days. When AT&T owned everything. You made your call. You got your bill.

Now you have to be a Ph.D. in math to possibly understand it.

Company #1 — You can call your ex-husband's sister-in-law in China for 2 cents a minute between 3:00 and 3:15 a.m. However, if you want to call your next door neighbor, read paragraph three.

Company #2 — You can have call waiting, caller I.D., call forwarding, and voice mail for a penny a minute, but if you don't want all of the above, read page sixteen.

As far as I'm concerned, caller I.D. is the worst invention of the twentieth century. I HATE that my sons-in-law know how many times a day I call my daughters.

I wanted to call one of my daughters the other day. First I had to check the time of day to try and figure out which one of the myriad activities she would be at. That was the easier part. I had to try and remember what her car phone number was, her cell number, her pager number and her work number. By the time I got all the numbers straight I totally forgot what I wanted to tell her!

Wasn't it only last week that I just opened the door and yelled, "Come in, I have to tell you something."

When you call a business you have to listen to, "We now have a new menu" and then they list twenty-five options. By the time you punch in what you want, your business transaction has escaped your mind.

I'm all for writing a letter, but what's that? Now it's e-mail or fax.

Anyone for charades?

Wear Glasses

I was dressing for a black-tie wedding on the hottest, most sticky day in over twenty years. We were in the country and going to drive into the city for the event.

I had exactly what I needed—nothing extra. My dress was long and slinky with a slit up to THERE. My shoes were spikes. Getting the shoes on even when my feet were dry was like Cinderella.

Shower, hair, makeup, jewelry—ready to dress. I took the panty hose out of the package and got a sinking feeling as they looked like they would fit Barbie. I put on my glasses and I broke out in a sweat as I read the package. Size P (petite).

The day before, I was in a rush and I also didn't have my glasses on. I grabbed the package thinking the P was an M, for medium. Now what was I going to do? It's Sunday in the country. No stores and no extra panty hose. I cannot wear a tight, slinky, slit dress

without hose and I will never get heels on without hose.
So I stretched and stretched and stretched one way and then I
stretched and stretched the other way.

Now time is going—time for the big moment. I put them on
and got them to my knees and STOP—they wouldn't budge a
millimeter.
I was frantic. So I did twelve knee bends and I grabbed ahold of
the waistband and jumped.

Like branches of a tree breaking were the sounds as I tore the
ligaments in my thigh.
I went to the wedding with flat shoes and holding my purse over
the slit.

When I was in the emergency room later, the attending physician
asked me how the accident happened.
"Well, Doctor, I was in a tennis tournament and I went for an over-head
and lost my balance."

Moral of the story is: Wear glasses when you purchase panty hose.

Movie set

During my "grandmother sitting week" I went for a walk around the development. It was a glorious day with each tree a more exquisite color. The homes are on an acre of land, with little ponds and forest preserves. I walked for two hours and never saw anyone who lived in the houses. I almost felt like I was on a movie set with fronts only. But there was laughter everywhere. The gardeners were singing away. Others were sitting or lying on the grass enjoying the scenery. Painters were kibbitzing, carpenters were eating lunch and the birds were singing.

The men of the households were busy earning a living, the women were also working or doing their thing, and the children were at school.

No one living in the houses to enjoy the beauty . . . only the people working on the houses.

Geometry

I don't get it. Why do you have to take geometry in high school if you are not going into a math-related field? The first day the teacher told us an L was a 90-degree angle. Those were the only words I ever comprehended after that, except "class dismissed!"

How to balance a checkbook and how to fill out a credit card application would be so much more helpful.

In Spanish class we memorized how to say, "The pen is blue" and "What is your name?" We should have learned to say, "Where's the nearest bathroom?" and "Can't you sell it a little cheaper?" In drama class we acted out the main Shakespearean roles. Better we should have studied how to say with conviction, "Yes, dear. You look VERY thin in that dress." and "Yes, dear. You look VERY tan."

Geometry

Instead of studying the latitude and longitude of a remote town in Timbuktu, why didn't they instruct us on the quickest route to the nearest mall?

Sewing class: What a waste! Why didn't they just give me a list of dressmakers?

Chemistry: Ridiculous if you're not going into the medical field. I would have loved to learn the minerals and properties of gemstones or the merits of Tylenol versus Advil.

Gym: Is it really important to swing from a ring and jump over a hurdle? Why couldn't I have been taught to play tennis or golf instead?

Sociology: Rather than study the people of Honolulu, why didn't they give us tips on how to get along with your in-laws and how to survive your teenagers?

Why couldn't they have suntan lamps instead of fluorescent lights? How can a kid get a tan sitting in a classroom all day?

Why doesn't school start at 10 A.M.? Everyone knows how crucial a good night's sleep is!

Why can't school end at one? We all know how important after school activities are!

Why isn't there a four-month summer vacation, May 1 through August 31? We all realize how vital it is that kids get fresh air and exercise.

Nutrition: Who needs to study that—unless it's your field? Better they should give us a list of all the restaurants in our area that deliver.

Health: We all understand how babies are born and the danger of AIDS by the time we reach high school. Instead they should tell us the benefits and costs of the area's health clubs.

Maybe if the educators heeded my advice, the drop-out rate wouldn't be so high.

A PLEASURE

I love to play tennis with my best friend. My husband could beat me with a blindfold on.

He loves playing tennis with me because I'm a pleasure to play with.

Of course I only play on the shade side. I can't stand it when the sun is in my eyes. Naturally, I stop every few minutes for water and rest. I certainly don't want to get leg cramps or become dehydrated.

All weather conditions are studied as carefully as a space launch. Not too cold, not too hot, not too humid, not too sunny, not too windy. If all conditions are A-OK, it's a GO!

I love to volley as long as he doesn't aim for my face or body and he hits the ball about 8 inches to my right—never to my left.

I love to rally. Of course my husband has to abide by my rules.

No shots down the line.

No shots crosscourt.

No drop shots.

No overheads.

Never, ever a backhand.

No slice on the ball.

No spin on the ball.

Not too deep.

No smashes.

I want a nice simple shot to my forehand. Of course, I'm allowed to put the ball away and do whatever I wish with it.

I'm such a pleasure to play with.

Tennis, anyone?

It's ridiculous

Bananas—super for you—loaded with potassium.
Bananas—horrible for you—loaded with carbs.

Watermelon—terrific for you—natural diuretic.
Watermelon—terrible for you—all sugar.

Bacon-great—no carbs.
Bacon-bad—all fat.
Slim-Fast—The Zone—Weight Watcher's—Jenny Craig—Suzanne
Sommers—Atkins—Sugar Busters—my brain is spinning.

I cannot digest (excuse the pun) anymore information on what
food group to eat or to avoid. Everything is either loaded with fat,
carbohydrates, sugar or sodium. It's a beautiful day, but I can't fill
up on air.
You need a little fat—you must eliminate all fat.

I've had it. I will not listen to the TV news health report so tomorrow I can hear about the dangers of an apple.

I will not read another newspaper article about foods so I'll learn about some invisible bug that lives in lettuce.

If I eat the same amount of calories I expend, I will stay the same weight.
If I eat more calories than I expend, I will gain weight.
If I eat fewer calories than I burn off, I will lose weight.

End of sentence, finito, period.

I've had it. Do you hear me world? I WILL NOT BE SUCKED INTO LISTENING TO THIS WEEK'S DIET CRAZE.!

Wait a minute. TV's on. What did I just hear on "Oprah?" Something about a reward meal.

Turn that volume up!

LOOK, LOOK!

Thousands of tourists came to Chicago last summer to see the "Cows on Parade", a marvelous exhibit of dozens of plastic cows in different poses with varied themes up and down Michigan Avenue.

I was meeting two very chi-chi friends from New York who always look like the cover of Vogue magazine. I was looking through Neiman Marcus's fall catalog and saw the most stunning outfit. Black pants, a white and black sweater, a cow-print purse, and matching shoes. My fingers started reaching for the phone and I quickly dialed and ordered the entire ensemble.

I wore it to lunch yesterday and my friends couldn't stop raving how stunning my outfit was. I didn't have to be complimented. I knew what I was wearing was the latest style in all the fashion bibles.

After lunch we went walking on Michigan Avenue so they could see some of the cows. All of a sudden children started shrieking, "Look, look! The cow lady, the cow lady!" I looked in the direction they were pointing, but didn't see anyone. I then realized that they were all staring at me! I didn't know if I should laugh, cry or run.

While I was deciding what to do, two of the moms came over to me. I actually felt bad for them, as I knew they would be falling all over themselves apologizing for their rude offspring.

I braced myself and got ready to say, "Don't worry about it." Instead I heard, "Oh miss, you came to the city dressed like a cow lady. Wasn't that cute? Could we take a picture of you next to the cow with our kids?"
I wanted to scream, "I'm not from out of town and I'm not the cow lady! I live a block away and this outfit is on page 37 of Neiman's catalog!"

Instead, I put my arms around the children, stood next to the cow, and smiled weakly.

U.P.S.

SUN.   Years ago the only place you could get New York cheesecake was in New York.
My husband went there for a business trip and the first
thing he did was to follow my instructions.

MON.   Go to Lindy's and send me a cheesecake. And indeed he
did. It arrived on Tuesday morning.

TUES.   I tore open the package and quickly devoured a slice,
with skim milk of course. I put the rest in the freezer for the weekend when we were having a big party.

WED.   I had to try a piece from the freezer. I had to make sure
that it still had the same taste when it was frozen.

THURS. Refrigerator empty and who wants to go shopping in the
rain?

Breakfast — cheesecake
Lunch — cheesecake
Dinner — cheesecake
Snack — cheesecake
Being the concerned wife that I was, I cut a generous slice for my husband and put it in the back of the freezer for him.

FRI.   Baby has temperature. Can't leave house, so I repeated the menus of the day before.

FRI. Night One piece left—his piece in the freezer. But wait, I thought, do I want my husband to eat all that cholesterol and consume all those calories? Absolutely not! So I very nicely ate it for him.

FRI. NIGHT   "Hi sweetheart. I'm home. Missed you. Love you."

VERY LATE

"Let's have some coffee, cheesecake and catch up on the kids."
"What cheesecake? It never came." "It never came? Why didn't you tell me?" "I didn't think you had time to order it." "Honey, I'm so sorry it got lost. I'll call U.P.S. in the morning."

It's twenty years later and they are still looking.

ANGEL DUST

I was cleaning the closets recently and came across boxes of wigs. Long and straight, long and curly, short with bangs, page-boy, and all of Cher's styles.

I swear there is a magic mirror in stores. Over the years, I will innocently be walking by the wig department and a saleslady will grab me and implore me to just "try it on."

I put the wig on, look into the mirror, and I'm transformed. I'm Cher—opening night in Vegas. I feel so glamorous and look so gorgeous that I'm thinking of leaving my husband and kids and flying to Hollywood. The whole world should see me. I now have a small crowd of women around oohing and aahing how terrific I look and urging me to buy it.

I didn't need any pressure; I couldn't whip out my charge card quick enough.

An hour later, I'm home and I couldn't wait to put my flowing hairpiece on. I adjusted it, looked in the mirror and screamed. It was Halloween in August. I was a witch, Dracula and a female Frankenstein all rolled into one. I just needed a broom to complete what a hideous horror I had become. I quickly cancelled my flight to L.A. as I pondered what magic they sprinkle on department store mirrors.

THE CIRCLE

My grandmother never received any love. Her parents' time and energy just went into survival. When she was sixteen, she was sent off to America to become a maid. Her marriage to my grandfather was arranged by a matchmaker. She lived in a loveless marriage, so she never knew how to show any love to my mother. Her father adored her, though, and my mother was showered with love and affection.

I could never adequately express in words the constant adoration and nonjudgmental love I got from my mother. I miss her so much every day. My mother's hobbies, vacation and avocation were her daughters and granddaughters.

I know that I learned to love and care for my daughters with every fiber of my being from my mother. She always wanted everything to be perfect in the family and everything to go smoothly in her "job". I know when I try to settle things or want everyone to get along, my girls think I am interfering or overreacting. But it's my mother's voice that speaks to my heart.

My greatest daily joy is seeing what kind of wonderful mothers my daughters are to their children. Like my mom, like me, they are consumed with their accomplishments, their disappointments, and every happening of their day. They show them love all day in every way.

The circle will be complete when they see all the love and devotion their children will foster on their children.
I'm going to go pop a vitamin pill because I want to be here to see it.

I love you all so much.

Mom

GROW BABY GROW

My husband flew on Monday to Beverly Hills on business and
I was to join him on Friday.

Monday night he called and said, "Honey, I was walking on
Rodeo Drive today and all the women are sooo skinny. See if you
can lose ten pounds by Friday."

"Sweetheart," I said, "I was walking on Michigan Avenue today
and all the men were sooo tall. See if you can grow six inches
by Friday."

Bye, dear."

MILLIONS

We spent a wonderful weekend in Las Vegas. I had the flu a
week before and as we were packing to go home, my husband
was telling me how badly he felt when I was under the weather.

"Honey," he said, "I can't stand it when you don't feel well, or
if something is bothering you emotionally or physically."
I had about fifteen minutes more of packing, so I told him to
go to the casino and I would meet him at the crap table.

I started to pack my toiletries. I tried to close a glass jar of makeup, but it was not tightening correctly. So I turned it with all my
might. The glass shattered; a piece sliced across my wrist and
the blood spurted out.

I quickly wrapped a towel around my wrist and ran to the phone.
"Operator, my wrist is accidentally slashed. Please send
a doctor immediately to room 2480."

"All right ma'am, stay calm, I will connect you to security."
"I don't want security. I have not been robbed or raped. I want
a doctor."
"Very well, ma'am, I will connect you to security."

I realized that while they filed their security report, I would
bleed to death. So with the white towel turning red, I ran for
the elevator.

By the time the elevator arrived, went down twenty-four floors,
and I found my husband in the vast casino, I felt faint. I really was-
n't thinking of myself, though. All I could think about was how dis-
traught he was going to be. He would take one look at me and
probably faint himself.

"Honey," I said, "stay calm, don't panic, but I'm bleeding very
badly and need to go to the emergency room." I needn't have
worried about his reaction to my injury as he had the dice and his
eyes never left the table. He kept chanting, "The table is
hot. The table is hot."

"Honey, I have the dice. I have money on every number and
every number is pressed and double pressed. Here's $100.
Take a cab or limo. Love you."

"Take me now!" I yelled. "I probably need a transfusion!" He
reluctantly, under great duress, left the table and took me to the
hospital.

He's convinced to this day that if I had let him stay at the table and not dragged him away, he would have made millions.

MONDAY MORNING

Called the airlines—put on hold
Called a doctor—put on hold
Called the plumber—put on hold
Called the beauty shop—put on hold
Called about theater tickets—put on hold
Called newspaper delivery—put on hold
Called the insurance company—put on hold
I keep hearing the message: "Your business is important to us." If
it's so important, why don't they answer my call?!
So I called a friend to chat and was put on hold.
I called my daughters and they all put me on hold.
I called my husband and he put me on hold.
WON'T ANYONE SPEAK TO ME?!

WHERE, OH WHERE

Where or where have my glasses gone?
Have you seen my car keys?
You're sure you didn't see my glasses?
I can't find my purse!
I just put my glasses down a minute ago!
Have you seen my house keys?
Darn it, I left my umbrella in the cab!
Where are my GLASSES?!
Oh no, I lost another pair.

My daughter says I need a keeper. I was leaving the house quickly and decided to hide my jewelry. I've done this in the past, and when I get home from a trip I can't remember where I hid my baubles.

Where, oh where

This time, though, I was smart and organized. I wrote myself a note describing where they were.

Now, if I can only locate my glasses, I'm going to try to find the note. Where could they both be?

Counting Sheep

As the millennium approached we did not count sheep as we were trying to fall asleep. Instead we all conjured up our millennium resolutions.

I will start a diet January 1, 2000.

I will exercise every day.

I will eat correctly.

I will take vitamins.

I will give more money to charity.

I will donate time to a worthwhile cause.

I will visit older, lonely relatives.

I will learn or improve my skills at a sport or musical instrument.

I will read more, learn a foreign language, take a course.

I will be more patient, more compassionate, more forgiving, etc., etc., ad infinitum.

Of course, January 1 comes and you're exhausted from New Year's so you can't possibly get up and exercise.

Counting sheep

You're invited to a New Year's brunch where the hostess spent hours creating delicious, delightful delectables that would be so rude to refuse.

One of the guests handed you sheets of the latest jokes on the Internet, so of course there's no chance to open your new novel.

You're anxious to see if anyone is going to win tonight on "Who Wants To Be A Millionaire?", so you'll watch educational TV tomorrow.

Tomorrow, of course, the real world begins again with all its responsibilities, problems, and pressures.

Oh well, we all had good intentions—back to counting sheep.

The Ultimate House Gift

Neighbors of ours were having friends from L.A. for a week's visit. The parents were also bringing their three little toddlers. My friend was looking forward to their stay, but she also knew how exhausted she would be at the end of the time.

A week later, I knocked on her door to see if she survived. While I was waiting for her to answer the door, I mentally pictured how she would look. I knew she would have bags under her eyes from having three babies underfoot all day and night.

My neighbor opened the door and my mouth fell open. She not only didn't look worn out, she actually looked ten years younger! "My God, what did you do?"
"Well," she said, "our friends brought the perfect house gift. No plants, candy, fruit, CDs, crystal, or wine. He is a plastic surgeon and he brought me botox and collagen."

The ultimate house gift

We also have guests arriving soon, and our friend is also a doctor, but my luck—he's a proctologist!

HIS WORST NIGHTMARE

My husband needed extra help at his showroom due to a moving sale. So his worst nightmare came to fruition when I offered to help, and actually showed up and stayed.

Of course, after one hour on the job, I wanted to change every tried and true system because I was convinced that I knew a better and more efficient way of doing things. With each suggestion his face got redder, and I'm sure he was making a concerted effort not to clench his fist.

I knew I was quickly wearing out my welcome in the office so I decided to help people in the showroom.

1st woman: I have a broken part I would like to return.
Me: I will be happy to get someone from customer service to help you. I don't deal with that.

2nd woman: I paid this invoice and I keep getting a statement.
Me: I will be happy to get someone in billing to help you. I don't deal with that.

3rd woman: I would like to know if my order was shipped out.
Me: I will be happy to call the shipping department and they'll talk to you. I don't deal with that.

4th woman: Excuse me, but I overheard you; what exactly do you deal with?
Me: Well, madam, I am in charge of the happiness department. I take orders and take money. Since I'm not getting paid, I created a department that will only give me happiness!

Everyone burst out laughing, and for a moment they all looked happy.

I'LL TEACH YOU A NEW WORD

When we go to Vegas, I don't gamble. If I'm going to spend money, I want a credit card in my right hand and a shopping bag in my left.

After standing and watching my husband for two hours, I was starting to get a little bored. At 11 P.M. there was not an option of the four S's—sun, swimming, shopping, or spa. The fifth S . . . well, we already know he was at the casino.

"When in Rome do as the Romans do," so I took $100 and walked over to a slot machine. I went to what was called a progressive machine. A million dollar jackpot and RISING!

I put $3 in and $200 came out. A guard was standing next to the machine and said "It's your lucky night, lady."

You are right, sir, and I'm going to teach you a new word. The word is schmuck. It is Yiddish and it means stupid, dumb, idiot, numbskull. I am an intelligent woman and I put $3 in and a couple hundred came out. So since I have a brain, I will clutch the money to my chest and leave ahead of the game. A schmuck would stand here, throw away all his winnings plus more, because he stupidly thinks he will win the jackpot."

I walked away with my little hoard feeling very smug. Gloating actually. You gamble a few bucks, you win, you walk. What discipline and control I possess. Why can't I be this controlled over a chocolate eclair?

As I got in the elevator I had a startling thought. There was $1 million, probably a $1,100,000 jackpot on that machine. The casinos aren't lying, there has to be a payoff or they would lose their license. Someone has to win. Now why shouldn't it be me?

So I pressed the down button and went back to the same slot machine.

Click, click, click. I put in the remaining $97 from my first hundred.

Click, click, click. I put in all the winnings.

Click, click, click. I put in another $100. Alas, the lights did not start to flash and I did not become an instant millionaire.
The same guard was standing there and I went over, stuck out my hand and said, "Sir, shake hands with a schmuck."

SALUTE

I walk in the morning in a park that is filled with statues. Not
George Washington, John Kennedy, or Martin Luther King Jr. I'm
sure these were all very brave men. However, I never heard of
them; they were in battles I never read of, in places I was not
aware of.

If I designed a park, there would be a large black sculpture of a
pair of pull-on elastic-waist pants with a plaque of the name of
the person who thought up this brilliant idea.

Further down would be a sculpture of fudge Snackwell's cookies
with a plaque to their inventor.

The center of the park would have a huge statue of Donna Karan
wearing a black unitard, black wrap skirt, and black control top
opaque panty hose.

Next would be a huge can of Diet Coke.

Last, but not least, would be a sculpture of a workout bra. Believe me, as the women of the neighborhood jogged, walked, pushed the strollers, biked, or roller-bladed by, they would all bow, salute, or curtsy.

OUT OF THE MOUTHS OF BABES AND OTHER RANDOM THOUGHTS

One of my grandsons, age ten, is a chocoholic. He's naturally slim, or so I thought. He's also an athlete who has to "make weight" at some of his sports tournaments.

We were spending the day together and we walked by a chocolate candy store. "Come on, let's go in and I'll buy you a few pieces."

"Absolutely not, Grandma. Thanks anyway."

"But why? You love chocolate!"

"Grandma, I already know what that candy tastes like. Why waste the calories when I know the taste?"

I've asked him to tape that thought, so I can send my brain a subliminal message while I sleep.

I was discussing with my thirteen-old grandson what he thinks he wants to do when he's an adult. "Well, Grandma, you know as a little boy I always wanted to be president. But then I decided I couldn't live with the fear of assassination. So I decided to be a baseball manager, but after thinking it over, there's not any job security and you are away from your family for too long. So I made my final decision. I want a career where I can use my brains, make a lot of money, and help people. I'm going to become a doctor."
"That's wonderful dear. Do you know what field of medicine?"
"Yes, Grandma, breast implants."

We were watching "Oprah" on television one day, and the topic of her show was diets. Doctors were advocating sometimes eating dessert first. Although I couldn't quite figure out the advantage, I said, "Gee, that sounds like a good concept."
The eleven year old piped up and said, "Grandma, what's so new about that idea? You have always eaten dessert first!"

I took my favorite granddaughter (only one) to American Girl for the day. We were looking forward to a wonderful lunch as the waiter approached our table with the food. He then proceeded to give my granddaughter her grilled cheese, french fries, chocolate sundae and cake. He gave me the Caesar salad, fresh fruit, and diet coke. I gave my granddaughter a "Don't speak!" look. I waited until the server had walked back into the kitchen before I switched our lunches!

I took our three-year-old grandson to F.A.O. Schwarz to see all the new exhibits and to buy him a toy. We left thirty minutes later and he sobbed all the way home.

No, it was not because I changed my mind and wouldn't buy him anything. No, it was not because what he wanted was too expensive. No, it was not because what he wanted was not appropriate for his age or too bulky to carry. He was crying because he wanted to get a toy, and EVERY toy in the store that would interest a three-year-old boy he already had.

I love sports—not only to participate in, but to watch. But I think baseball is B-O-R-I-N-G. Unless, of course, my grandsons are up at bat or pitching. I'd rather read a book or be doing what I am now, writing instead of watching Sammy Sosa or Mark McGuire. However, my twelve-year-old grandson star pitcher eats and breathes baseball. He actually reads the baseball statistics as he eats his cereal in the morning. So forget the editorials and fashion pages. I, too, now read the latest baseball news so he'll think I'm cool and my conversation will interest him. If you can't beat 'em, join 'em!

My grandson and granddaughter were misbehaving and they were sent upstairs. In their bedrooms and upstairs playroom are their computers, telephones, stereos, CDs, TVs, hundreds of tapes, Nintendo games, books, toys, and two birds. Some punishment, to go to their rooms! But I guess some things never change. Many years ago, my dad decided that the whole family, including the grandchildren, should paint the pool. He would save a lot of money and he thought the kids would enjoy it.

"Girls", he said, "go inside and change your clothes. Put on some old stuff and we'll start."

Five minutes later, my daughters all came running out of the house, crying. "Grandpa, we can't help you paint," they said. "We don't have any old clothes. Everything still has a tag on it."

My husband was hitting tennis balls to our three-year-old grandson. Each ball came back over the net. Soon a crowd had gathered and people were yelling, "Look out, Sampras!" I thought to myself, he's probably the only three year old who understands how to hit a solid forehand and not swing the racquet like a baseball bat, but cannot comprehend "going to the potty". I hope by the time he gets to Wimbledon, he'll be toilet trained.

My five-year-old grandson was telling me the other day how you can pick the sex of your child. If you want a boy, you eat grape-fruit all day and if you want a girl, you eat salads all day. Somehow his scientific evidence is off, as I have three daughters and never eat lettuce.

Did I hear right?

You need a little fat
You need a little fat
Honestly, this is what I heard on "Oprah", as I sat on my
yoga mat.

You need a little fat
You need a little fat!
Those words jingled in my ears when I ran, and even when I sat.

You need a little fat
You need a little fat?
For this diet plan I'll go to bat.

You need a little fat
You need a little fat
Bacon, cheese, and steak, I digested all the fat.

Did I hear right?

"Enjoy, enjoy," my husband said (dubiously), as he gave my
tush a pat.

You need a little fat
You need a little fat
Maybe it worked on the experiments with rats.
But on me, all those lipids turned to fat, fat, fat.

So I'm shutting out that tune and made up my own little jingle.

You've got to give up a little
If you want to lose a little

You've got to starve a while
You've got to run the extra mile

You've got to think thin
Eating junk food is a sin

Carbs are so bad for you
You are just allowed to have a few

You've got to give up a little
To lose a little

Somehow, I think the C.D.
You need a little fat
You need a little fat
Is going to sell much better than mine.

The Broken-Down Truck

Many years ago, my brother-in-law was in law school and my sister was working to support them. My husband, being older, was already established in his own business. I knew it was not an easy time for them financially, and I made a concerted effort not to discuss with them purchases we made.

One December weekend, my husband and I went to New York for a business trip. I was very excited because we had just had our third and last child, and I was finally going to get rid of all the maternity clothes and buy a new wardrobe.

Since there wasn't a F.A.O. Schwarz toy store in Chicago then, I suggested to my husband that we buy the children their holiday gifts from Schwarz's in New York. We also buy a large amount of corporate gifts, and I thought it would really look nice for clients to see that we took the time and effort to purchase their gifts in the big apple.

The broken-down truck

So between all my purchases, the children and family holiday
presents, and corporate gifts, there were a lot of packages.
I shipped everything home to avoid paying the state tax, and
not have to schlep all the presents home.

When I came back, my sister and I were discussing the trip and
she asked if I bought anything. "Yes, I did," I said, "a pair of shoes
and a purse." I really didn't feel comfortable discussing the purchases we had made.

While we were talking, a U.P.S. truck pulled up to the house.
Oh no! I thought quickly, though, and asked my sister to check on
the children. I ran outside and said to the driver, "When you come
in, please say that the truck's brake lights are on and you have to
bring it into a gas station. Say you're not allowed to leave a truck
with merchandise, so could you please unload the packages in
our house."

When my sister came downstairs a minute later and said, "My
God, where did all this stuff come from?" the driver repeated the
story.

A few years later when her husband became very successful,
I told her the truth and we laughed at the story I concocted.

THE SEARCH

I was babysitting for my grandchildren. Marathon sitting to be
exact—two whole weeks. One night an apple or diet gum for
a snack just didn't cut it. So I went on a search for something
sweet. My grandchildren only like salty products, so the cabinets
and cupboards were filled with Cheetos, Fritos, and potato
chips—all items I could easily resist. I wanted sugar. SUGAR.
SUGAR.

I waited until they were sound asleep, and I tiptoed into their
room looking for their Halloween candy. (This was the middle
of January, by the way.) The door started to squeak and I
jumped back, afraid I would be caught. I waited until their
breathing was deep and even, and I tiptoed in again. I grabbed
the pumpkin basket and quickly escaped. A few Tootsie Rolls and
I was a happy camper. Everything else in the basket
(Thank God!) I hated.

The search

A few days later I needed another fix, but this time there was a big fat ZERO in the house. However, a lightbulb went on! Their Lunchables were in the refrigerator. For those of you who don't have small children, a Lunchable is a small package containing mini lunchmeats, nachos or crackers, and two cookies. As carefully as if I were cracking Tiffany's diamond safe, I opened each package* and stole the cookies. However, I now had a big problem. How do I fill the empty space? So I took packages of Gummy Bears, filled in the open slots and re-taped them.

My granddaughter did not say anything for ten days. One morning she finally asked, "Grandma, where did you buy my Lunchables with the Gummy Bears? All the kids in my class are begging their moms to buy them. Their mothers go from store to store searching, and they can't find them!"

"Well, dear, sit down and I'll tell you a story, if you 'pinky promise' not to tell your mother or your friends."

*I REFUSE to tell you how many!

200 DEGREES

When my husband asked my father for my hand in marriage,
my dad of course told him that he was the luckiest guy on Earth
to marry me. But then he said, "I must warn you, my daughter will
burn your money faster than you can make it."

At one of my showers we received a large plastic piggy bank. We
soon got in the habit of throwing our change in there at
the end of the day. Before too long the bank was filled with
hundreds of dollars. We were living at the time in a suite hotel with
maid service.

We were leaving for the weekend and I was concerned about
the bank because the rooms were cleaned on Saturday. I put the
bank inside the stove because I knew
the maid never cleaned the inside unless I requested it.

200 degrees

A few days later we returned home. I unloaded the groceries and turned the oven dial to 200 degrees to preheat it for a roast. We went out for a walk and came back later to the horrific smell of burning plastic.

My husband ran to open the windows and turn on the fans as I ran to the oven. The huge plastic bank had baked into a pizza.

We sat for hours every night with a hammer and a chisel to no avail. Chopping, chopping trying to get the change loose. What I couldn't understand was why my husband wasn't shocked and furious.

"Honey," he said, "your dad told me you would burn my money. It was my mistake not taking him seriously."

BUSTED

My daughter, after much deliberation and much begging from
her husband and two sons, purchased a dog.

They bought a King Charles Royal Cavalier, based on the fact
that the animal is soft, cuddly, obedient, and most importantly
of all, never, ever barks.

I've been there when the phones are ringing, the doorbells are
buzzing, and the kids are wrestling. Dutch never moves a
muscle. The kids jump up and down on the trampoline and
he remains like a stuffed animal.

A few nights later, I slept over and woke up for my midnight feed-
ing. The house was quiet, everyone was sleeping and I had to
navigate my way downstairs in the darkness. I tiptoed down
the stairs feeling my hands along the wall until I got to the

pantry. I found the Oreos and as I bit into one, Dutch woke
up and began barking like the Russians were invading the house.

Meanwhile upstairs my hysterical daughter is yelling at my son-in-
law to call 911. "Someone has broken in," she was screaming.
"Dutch is hysterical."

"Calm down," he said. "It's your mother making a midnight raid."

"My mother is sound asleep," she said. "How dare you say that!
Call the police right now!!!"

"I suggest you check on your mother first," he said. So with a glar-
ing look at her husband she went to my room and realized
I was the cause of Dutch's hysterics.

I will not speak to that animal ever again for busting me!

HALT

The world has come to a halt. Everyone just sits and cradles a telephone while they are put on hold. I think the only people actually doing anything are the robot answering machines. All the living, breathing people are just holding, holding, holding.

Help

My husband and I took our daughter and her children to Disneyland. By the end of the day we had consumed enough pizza, hot dogs, and ice cream to feed a Third World country. We had walked miles and stood in endless lines. If I heard "It's a Small World After All" one more time, I would throw up!

All we wanted was a hot shower, peace and quiet, and a bed. We checked in, plopped on the bed, and welcomed the silence. It was short-lived however, because a fight broke out in the next room.

One kid was crying, one kid was screaming, and the mother was yelling the loudest of all. As the minutes went by, they didn't quiet down; the noise only escalated. We tried putting pillows over our heads, but nothing helped; the people in the next room kept getting more obnoxious.

Finally, we couldn't take it anymore. We grabbed the phone and asked for the desk clerk. "Please, sir," I said. "We need to have our room moved immediately. The people next door are keeping us up all night and they are giving us a headache. Put us on another floor."

"But madam," he said, "the people in the next room you're talking about are your children."

"Don't you think I know that?! Get me away from them!"

Higher education

I was playing singles with a woman I had just met. We had lunch and talked about ourselves. She explained that she really couldn't relax during the game, as it was her first day of retirement. She had worked since high school and had no idea how to "smell the roses."

"I have a Ph.D. in computer science," she said.

"You know," I replied, "we are going to form a partnership. You have a Ph.D. in computers, but you have no concept how to enjoy life. I also have a Ph.D. Mine stands for 'Princess of the Highest Dynasty.' However, I have no concept of how a computer works.
So here's the deal. I'll teach you how to be a princess and you'll teach me about computers."

"It's a deal," she said and we shook hands.

I CAN'T STAND IT

I can't stand when my grandchildren are:
Yelled at
Punished
Reprimanded
Ever said no to
Refused seconds for dessert
Told to be quiet
Told to straighten their room
Told to do their homework
Told to help around their house
Given a budget amount at Toys R Us

If I had my way, they would sit on a throne with me waiting on them while I plied them with kisses and heaped presents at their feet.

I can't stand it

God, I pray my sons-in-law don't read this. They will move my daughters to Australia on the next flight!

Not That Bad

My husband was hospitalized for some tests and he was not allowed even a sip of water.

After two days he was told he could eat and he had a yearning for a cinnamon roll. So my daughter was dispatched to the nearest bakery and she came back with two—one for me and one for him. She took them out of the bag and the first was small, dried out, had no frosting and was at least a day old. The second was fresh, HUGE, and dripping with frosting.

"Please Mom," said my daughter, "give Dad the good one."

I looked over and said, "Honey, he's not that sick," as I bit into the delicious one. "Plus the fact if I ate the dried one, he would really be worried there was something wrong with him."

Oh No

Many years ago when the children were little, we were at our
country house during Labor Day weekend. It was pouring on
Friday morning and there were dark clouds and cold weather
forecast for the weekend. The kids were upset that they couldn't
swim. My father suddenly had a brainstorm. "I'll drive to a fish
farm," he said, "and I'll buy a couple hundred trout and bring
them back in water and oxygen tanks. Invite all your friends
and neighbors over for a fish fry"

So we went to work. We called everyone we knew and told them
to bring fishing poles and bait. We set up chairs and newspapers
all around the pool. Everyone was saying that my father was nuts;
but we drain the pool after the holiday, so if he was willing to go
to all this effort—terrific.

We passed the time by making fish bets. Who would catch the first? Who would catch the biggest? Who would catch the most? And who would get the booby prize for coming up blank?

After my dad drove a few hours and spent hundreds of dollars, he arrived. By this time there were well over one hundred people around the pool. The children were all jumping up and down; they couldn't believe that they were going fishing in a pool. The dads were excited about catching fresh rainbow trout and the women were planning the fish dinners.

Two guys wheeled over the two fish tanks and they poured the 150 trout into the pool. A minute later everyone gasped and yelled, "Oh no!" as the fish instantly died. My dad forgot the pool was filled with chlorine!

I will spare you the story of how we got them out.

Passé

I was walking down Oak Street beach the other day and I
noticed a phenomenon. Did you read the word I used? Walking.

I was surrounded by hundreds of people and for a few minutes,
I was actually the only person I saw walking.
People were:
Jogging
Bicycling
Roller-blading
On scooters
On motorcycles
Swimming
Rowing boats
On jet skis
In horse and buggy
Waterskiing
On sailboats

On motorboats
On the trolley
In cabs
In cars
In limos
In buses
Laying on the sand
Sitting in lounges
Playing Cards
In wheelchairs
Pushing strollers
On adult tricycles
Jumping rope
Doing aerobics
Stretching
Reading
Playing chess
Eating
Drinking
Talking
Throwing Frisbees
Building sand castles
And playing volleyball

Is walking now passe?

SHUT UP

It's been said that you can tell a lot about a person's personality on the golf course or driving a car. Well, I say a fellow's behavior on the tennis court tells all.

A bad shot brings on:
I didn't sleep last night.
I have a blister on my finger.
This tennis elbow kills!
God, this sun is blinding me!
Did you ever see such winds?
The noisy people on the next court distracted me.
Are these balls any good?
I can't see without my visor.
I forgot my sunglasses.
Can't run—my knee hurts
The humidity is fogging my glasses.
I didn't have a chance to warm up.

I can't stand this new racquet.

And the all-time world-class comment:

I CAN'T RETURN HER BALL; SHE DOESN'T HIT WITH ANY PACE!

Has anyone thought of saying, "What a lousy shot I just hit!"?

Straight Out of Paris

I was straightening my closet and drawers and there were sweaters and lingerie everywhere. Things were piled on top of each other as I was trying to clean up the mess.

I realized I was late to meet my husband, so I threw a sweater over my pants, grabbed a coat, and ran out. When we got to the restaurant and I took off my coat, the attendant just gaped at me.

We sat down at dinner and after a few minutes everyone was staring at me. I couldn't figure it out and began to get very uncomfortable. There were several kids who were looking at me and giggling. I knew my sweater wasn't open because it was a turtleneck.

"OK", I thought, "I'll go to the bathroom and inspect myself." I walked into the ladies room and burst out laughing. A black lace bra was hooked to my sweater and laying on my right shoulder. My husband, sitting on my left, couldn't see it. I didn't know whether to take it off and spoil everyone's fun or emerge looking normal. "Anyone can look 'normal' " I thought, "I've got a great act going here." But I lost my nerve, unhooked the bra, and tucked it into my purse.

The Introduction

I was introduced to someone recently and I said my name was DIDYACAL. "Is that Polish or Hungarian? What is the origin of your name?" she asked.

"American," I answered. It stands for DID YOU CALL. As soon as my husband kisses me hello, he starts with DIDYACAL the kids, DIDYACAL the plumber, DIDYACAL the electrician, etc., etc., etc.

So now instead of saying Shana, my nickname, did you call _____, I officially changed my name to DIDYACAL.

THE LATEST

We were in the country for the weekend and I had brought only items we needed for our stay.

On Sunday night we were going to a black-tie wedding several hours away. It was a gorgeous day and I waited until way past the last possible moment to take a shower.

After wetting my hair, with my eyes closed I reached for the tube of shampoo. The consistency felt a little strange to me, but I was in too much of a rush to really pay attention.

That is until I tried to scrub my hair. I opened my eyes and realized I had not used shampoo. One of my daughters had put a deep, deep hair repairing conditioner in the shower. It felt like ten layers of Vaseline mixed with mud.

The latest

Thinking it was shampoo, I had put a handful on my hair instead
of just a dot, which the bottle of conditioner recommended.

I rinsed and rinsed to no avail. If I did not get out of the shower
immediately, I would miss the wedding. What was I going to do? I
was in the country. I didn't have a hat or a scarf. I had
no time to shop and there weren't any stores around anyway.

"Oh well," I thought, "go for it all the way." I dried the thick gob,
put actual Vaseline on my hair and slicked it back.

The wedding was in a small church outside Milwaukee.
The bride was one of my father's employees. As we lived in
downtown Chicago, the people in this little town thought we
were really 'big city slickers'.

So with my shoulders back and a confident smile, I strode into the
church. Of course, everyone stared at my grease ball of hair.

Soon after, the reception began and I was surrounded by all
the women. "Your hair is so chic," "Your hairstyle is so avant-
garde," "Your hairdo is fabulous," etc., etc., etc.

"Thank you," I said to one and all, "it's the latest out of Paris!"

WHO SAID WHAT

My teenage grandson and I were riding in a convertible on a beautiful, hot sunny day.

First person: "What a great day! Let's put the top down."
Second person: "Absolutely not! I don't want to mess my hair."
First person: "Let's at least open the windows and get some fresh air."
Second person: "No! It's too windy! It will mess my hair!"

Who said what?

You're wrong! WRONG! I wanted the top down!

You can't tell

You can easily tell where a person is from without speaking to them. All you have to do is notice what they are carrying or doing—it is a dead giveaway.

Tokyo—camera
Hong Kong—cell phone
Australia—newspaper
Canada—hockey stick
Venice—inner tube
Holland—tulip
Rome—guide to churches
Israel—dancing
Egypt—riding a camel
Hawaii—lei
China—everyone dressed alike
Scotland—golf clubs
England—umbrella

U.S.A.—jogging shoes and a bottle of water

Russia—vodka

Paris—holding hands

Caribbean—baskets on heads

Austria—croissant

Belgium—chocolate

Rio—suntan lotion

Bahamas—Panama straw hat

Athens—women swagger; men leer

Switzerland—skis

Mexico—Pepto-Bismol

Tahiti—looking for Marlon Brando

Cuba—searching for a boat to escape

Denmark—walking a dog

Mars—they are all walking around saying, "Do you think there is life on Earth?"

ROMANTIC INTERLUDE

In the forty years we have been going to our country house,
my husband and I have never been alone.

When we first married, the weekends were spent with my
parents and grandparents. Later, our daughters were in the
family circle. In the past thirteen years we have been blessed
to have our grandchildren there also.

But sometimes in the dark guilty part of our brains (after a
weekend of a few family disagreements), we would think about a
weekend alone.

Well, last month it actually happened. Everyone was busy
with other plans so my husband and I were going to have our
romantic interlude. On the drive up we talked about how we
would miss all the kids, but how relaxing, peaceful, and
romantic it would be.

We arrived and decided to take a swim together. No splashing, no yelling, no beach balls in our faces. Just two adults floating peacefully on pool lounges.

We each took hold of the pool cover and started to pull it back. I don't know who screamed louder. There was a huge dead raccoon floating in the pool. The animal must have fallen in and suffocated under the cover.

My husband doesn't like ants, so it was like he was confronted by a stampeding elephant.

"Call someone!" he screamed.

So I dialed:
Caretaker—Not home
Pool service—Out on calls
Police—Not their problem
Fire department—Not their problem
Animal control—In pool, our problem

It was windy, so by this time the gorilla is floating on its back—eyes glazed—up and down the pool while my husband stood FROZEN.

After all my calls to no avail, I told my husband to go to the neighbors for help. After a half hour, he came back very upset. He couldn't find anyone home.

"Can you believe it?" he said, "forty years we're here, surrounded by crowds of people and the one weekend we're alone, with no

one to help, there's a monster in the pool! Oh well, let's get
going. We have to take it out."

"Pardon me, dear," I said, "but there's no WE in this deal. It's you
and you alone!" With that, I ran in the house and locked
the doors.

My loving husband started screaming so loud he could be heard
in five surrounding states. "Your parents made you into a prima
donna and I've made you into a BIGGER PRIMA DONNA! A
PRIMA DONNA!!!!"

Meanwhile, I'm laughing so hard tears are running out of my
eyes. I quickly opened the door, threw out gloves, a broom,
and garbage bags, and locked the door.

Then as he was trying to lift the 1,000-pound tiger, he yelled,
"If this ever happens again, I'm out of this country house."

"Don't get lost going home, darling," I yelled back.

So much for our romantic interlude.

"THE BELLS ARE RINGING FOR ME AND MY GAL"

It was a lazy summer afternoon. I was doing my favorite activity-swimming, and my husband was doing his favorite-watching football.

All of a sudden I heard it. Was it my imagination, wishful thinking, or was it true? The sound grew louder as it came closer and closer. 'Honey, Honey, HONEY, HONEY! Come quick! HURRY, HURRY!" He ran outside not knowing if I had a cramp or was drowning.
"What happened? What's wrong?" he yelled.
"I hear it! I hear it!" I said.
"Hear what?" he said.
"The music!"
"What music?" he asked, "That's the football game that's on."
"No, no!", I said, "Listen! Don't you hear it, Pal? The bells are ringing for you and your gal. It's the ice cream truck! Hurry before it goes past!"

"The bells are rining for me and my gal"

"What are you talking about?!? It's the last quarter and the game is tied!!" he screamed.

"P-L-E-A-S-E! I didn't have lunch and I'm dying for an ice cream sandwich!" I pleaded.

"Fine," he said, with a dirty look as he took off jogging.

Twenty minutes later he came back. It seems as he went up one street, the ice cream truck turned the corner.

He stood there, huffing and puffing and dripping with sweat as he handed me my ice cream.

"But I HATE Neapolitan!" I cried.

Would you believe we're still married?

P IS FOR

I was proofreading some of my writings and realized that there is not a story about my mother.

I have been asking myself why, and the answer is I'm not gifted enough with words to write about her.

How do I write about an angel? When people first saw her they only exclaimed about her facial beauty. Once they knew her, it was how kind and wonderful she was. It seemed as if there was a halo of goodness around her head.

She carried the burdens of everyone on her shoulders. She would fret if a waitress looked tired or if the bus driver looked harassed.

Her days were spent tending to four different generations. She would run in the morning to help my dad in the office and bring him lunch. Then she would run with food to the nursing home for

her father. Then she would drive to the suburbs to see her daughters
and granddaughters and then she would run home
to tend to my grandmother who lived with them.

Her eyes lit up and she qvelled when she saw me. All she wanted
to do was please me and make me happy. I loved clothes. There
wasn't a cashmere at Marshall Field's Sunningdale Shop I didn't
have and I had enough formals to open a store.

She made me feel I was the most beautiful, smartest, and most
special girl in the world. But I know she made my sister and
her six granddaughters feel the same.

She never judged me and if she did, I was always right.
My husband laughs when I say, "What do you mean NO?!
My mother never uttered that word to me." She never, ever did.

She adored our three daughters and every spare moment she
was with them. My husband was the son she never had and they
were crazy about each other. We really were an extended family.
The only negative thing she ever said about him was that he
drove too fast.

My father, on the other hand, saw my sister and me with clear
vision. Whenever he said something negative or wanted to
punish us, my mother ran to defend us. That's why she was called
the D.A. (defense attorney).

Before I was married, I wrote copy for a suburban ad agency.
We lived in the city and it was quite a distance away.

I left for work one morning with the sun shining and a promise of a glorious day. By afternoon, though, a major storm hit the area. We had one car then and I remember thinking and hoping that my dad was not caught in an expressway jam due to the weather.

At 5:00 the receptionist called me and said that there was a drenched woman in the waiting room asking for me. I hurried out. It was my mother, who took a bus in the storm to bring me an umbrella.

So P is for perfection, my mother, Elizabeth Taylor on the outside, angel on the inside.

We never had an argument, but who could I ever tell that to? No one would believe me, except the fortunate people who knew her.

She touched the lives of everyone she saw on a daily basis. There were many "important" people at her funeral. But her elevator operator and the woman who shampooed her hair were there also.

I've just reread this and now I know why I've never written about my mother. I'm not capable of it. My words don't begin to describe the depth of her heart and the beauty of her soul.

So I'm giving up. All I know is that I miss her very much.

CALIFORNIA HERE I COME

I love California! But if you're thinking of moving there, believe me, it is not easy. The NC/BITS (Native Californians Born In The Sun) make it very difficult for aliens to enter their state.

If you're one of the thousands who are traveling cross-country on your way to the West Coast, here are a few tips to work on while you're driving:

1. When you enter the state, if your teeth are not white and straight, do not smile. Speak through clenched lips.

2. Wear a tennis skirt or golf outfit so you'll at least look the part.

3. Stop at every McDonald's and Burger King on your way across country and eat all the hamburgers and French fries you can possibly consume. Also try to swallow as much grass as you can so you can try and develop a taste for goat food, because

once you enter California, all they will allow you to eat is tofu, soy, and alfalfa.

4. Buy a book on golf and study and memorize every page. English is not spoken in California. They speak a language called Golfese (pronounced like Portuguese). Even if you hate golf and have no intention of ever playing, if you do not master the language you will have no one to speak to. Say to the border guard, "You know pal, I got a birdie on #5 at Cyprus yesterday with a 7 iron even though I shanked and had a bad lie coming up." You'll be given at least a B in Golfese.

5. Throw away all of your makeup before you get to California and get tattooed eyebrows, tattooed lips, and tattooed eyeliner. This will immediately impress the magnifying lens border guards.

6. Once you are at the border and they ask you what your profession is, never say plumber, teacher, salesperson, etc. They will find that too straight and boring. Say you either give steroid injections to palm trees, acupuncture shots to cats, or that you're a set designer at Warner Bros. Studios.

7. If you have short natural nails, keep your hands clenched until you can get to the nearest beauty shop and get tips or acrylics.

8. Glasses are as passe as the covered wagon, so get colored contacts or Lasik surgery. Do not, I REPEAT, DO NOT wear bifocals. You'll be turned back with no chance of ever entering again.

When you actually reach the border, there will be weighing guards at every point of entry. If you are more than three pounds over your ideal weight, you are turned back. The same goes for brunettes or redheads. No entry. Blondes or streaked blondes only. However, there are stands set up everywhere where you can purchase bottles of bleach or peroxide.

From there you will proceed to border station #2 where the tape measure guards will measure you. If you are flat chested, you must immediately go to a boob doctor for breast implants. You are given seven days notice to do this if you are not a 38D.

If you pass the first two points of entry, you are able to proceed to station #3 where the magnifying lens guards are positioned. Your face will be scrutinized and you will then be given a card stamped "Face lift", "Botox", "Collagen" or "Laser". You will be given two weeks to have the necessary surgery and if there is a financial problem, the state government will issue an interest-free loan.

From there you proceed to point #4, the therapy station. In Chicago, if you have a major crisis, you cry, wring your hands and beat your breast. In California, if you can't decide if you should wear a black or blue dress, you see a therapist. So at the border you must sign up for a male or female therapist and state how many times a week you want a session.

Next stop is the workout station. You are given athletic skills tests where they rate your abilities in golf, tennis, aerobics, Pilates, and yoga. You are then assigned what community you can live in so all the players will be equal in ability. If you are asked how high you hike or how far you can walk, just reply, "I have no idea, but I know I stopped in Scottsdale, Arizona, for a drink after my last jog from Chicago."

While you are going through this scrutiny you will notice water fountains everywhere. There are cameras positioned at the base of the fountain that will record your picture if you take a drink. Never, ever drink from a water fountain. Always carry your water bottle with you and pretend you are constantly popping vitamins, even if they are really M&Ms.

If, God forbid, shudder the thought, you do not workout, tell the athletics guard that you are recovering from a broken leg. This will give you six months to be retested and in that time you can learn a sport or hire a trainer and develop a respectable workout routine.

From there proceed to station #6, which is the relationship center. If you are in a relationship, never refer to the person you are involved with as your girlfriend, boyfriend, or significant other. At all times refer to that individual as your lover. If you have been married to the same person for over forty years, as I have, never admit it's to the same man. Say you've been married for forty years, but that you've had seven different husbands. When I innocently replied that I was married to the same man for forty years, my husband and I were immediately whisked to an emergency relationship helicopter and taken to a relationship sanitarium where they quarantined us to study our behavior. During our time there, we were issued red armbands that read "I've been married to the same person for over forty years".

You have now passed all points of entry. Congratulations! You will be issued a map of the state's 25,000 golf courses and a large bottle of instant bronzing suntan lotion.

If you fail, you have two options:

1. Turn around and head back to Kansas. Learn to love living in the dark. Try again in a year. This time leave the Ford Explorer at home and attempt to cross the border in a red Jag convertible.

2. You can enter the P.W.W.B.I.T.D. (People Who Were Born In The Dark) camp. There you will be attended around the clock by plastic surgeons, therapists, beauticians, Golfese instructors, trainers, and athletics coaches. In other words, everyone you need to get you into a I.W.N.B.H.B.I.T.T.F.I. (I Was Not Born Here But I'm Trying To Fake It) camp. When you are not studying for your degree, your spare time will be spent hunched over from planting palm trees and trying to stand up with your 44DDD breasts.

So now you know why I live in Chicago and am only allowed to vacation in California. The state flunked me in every category.

After reading all of my dirty little noshing secrets, I know you all think I'm a hippopotamus. I'm actually a loose, so loose, size 6 and should be a size 4 by the time this is in print—maybe even a 2*.

*Liar, liar. pants are on fire!